California Sorrow

California Sorrow

poems

Mary Kinzie

ALFRED A. KNOPF   NEW YORK   2007

THIS IS A BORZOI BOOK
PUBLISHED BY ALFRED A. KNOPF

www.randomhouse.com/knopf/poetry

A list of previously published poems appears on page 93.

Grateful acknowledgment is made to Deutsche Verlags-Anstalt for permission to translate
"Mit wechselndem Schlüssel" from *Von Schwelle zu Schwelle* by Paul Celan, copyright © 1955
by Deutsche Verlags-Anstalt, München. Reprinted by permission of Deutsche Verlags-Anstalt,
a division of der Verlagsgruppe Random House GmbH (Random House Germany).

Library of Congress Cataloging-in-Publication Data

Kinzie, Mary.
California sorrow : poems / by Mary Kinzie.—1st ed.
p. cm.
ISBN: 978-0-307-26680-4
I. Title.
PS3561.I59C35 2007
811'.52—dc22   2007020756

Manufactured in the United States of America
First Edition

Contents

California Sorrow

The Water-brooks

Slag and synthesis and traveling fire

so many ways the groundwaves of distortion
                                          pulse
            through bedrock   traffic   and the carbon chain
to be partitioned by result

particulate pollution   fine soot   fine biosolid dust   fine spark
                    of transuranium

water   out of breath   weighed down with nitrogen   water
        borne and water
                ruining toxins
                        tending to methane
                    and sulfuric   that eats the hulls off ships

gases from fuels that fume above the pavement   then in
        backburn from the rockets aimed into orbit
        falling down as watery
                        jet thrust   everlastingly
        degrading in a spittle of alpha particles

                breathed out as from a mouth half-open during sleep

                through the fetid afternoon
                        of future time

                                                Not to mention what
            they're hiding underground
                        down the unrenewable
                reamed veins of oil and ore
                                having siphoned out
                the water to leave new kinds of moisture
        bonded to killer molecules and the god-tick

of radioactivity

In time nothing will grow out here but spiny cardoon and yucca always
    already stunned into sterility

But the young
          the young on the highways now feel free as the breeze
      some with the windows down   the rust
        eating at the grille   the tailpipe lacy
    others with smoked windows and polysemous
          flames along the hood   or hubcaps
      with a sluggish glisten of foil paint
        to look like heavy alloy
    still others in cool models   gifts of parents   safety-heavy
        with large salaries beneath them

all weave in long inevitable ribbons   the young
    with the also rapid middle aged   and the elders
      rabid with longing that is a kind of greed
    and the truckers of unstoppable mileages
        and tonnage

all all

twine and re-form like sand moved by a whip
in a desert where soil is just a memory and the ground
    deep-stained   as are the cells   as is the
        air
        choked with an overcrossing
      threadwork of impurity
    about the heart and lungs
        over the
        aquifers whose downward plumes
    trickle toward each other

and the thirsty dangers spread

free as the breeze

Meanwhile the atmosphere so light you would not think
so many tons of lethal mist   gas   airborne speck   and effluent
could sit there
                    hooked upon the lightness that we breathe

Where still the Lockheed Martins
                              pictured on their website
          in the aching blue   silvery as needles
thread the sky with slubs
          of vaporous kerosene   (not pictured
                              yellow as farmyard fleece
          that wind up
                somewhere else but in the very
                        system with the trees and frogs
                              and greasy updraft from the local takeout
                        that is ours
                our system
                        closed with us within it
          the private garden   walled
                against derangement
                        hortus conclusus
          where a carpet of primulas once led from the virgin's hem
                to the flank of the reclining unicorn
                above the brook   should they be thirsty

          nowhere now to go

                   although

the pilots and the smelters and executive engineers
          ingenious destructive boyish and not scrupled
gasp with delight
          projected on the clouds they leave behind

These were the men who made the movies too and the movie queens
like the most famous childless icon   Isis of availability
whose nervously brief wit
                    could not sustain her when they dressed her up
                              in undressed attitudes
          and made her up with the lipstick that looked as if it smelled
                    like the enameled thimbles of pomade from France
          opening   as Luca Turin might write   on the yeasty topnote of a fresh
                              gaufrette
                    over a harsh residual
                              like piss on tar   cut through
                              by overwhelming funeral lily
Norman Mailer found it fetching
          and the Kennedys   who licked it off like honey

not her words were sweet but her surfaces and
          diminished hormones and pro forma
                    happy welcome until
          Arthur Miller got her up in black and wrote her into the
Nevada desert   goddess on a sand shell   her face
          frowning in soft focus
                    beneath her inkstroked lids   blond as a thistle

                    drying up

and driven tumbling   under the pillsmooth moon

Dusk   a frame of deceptive gold around each freeway lamp
          unholy halo of fine-ground debris
                    and sulfurous moisture
                                        and the   heat
                    of short-chain fatty acids from the animal farms
                              of Chino
          suspended in the clammy chill of not
                    entirely night

The closer you come to each light
       the dimmer
           it seems to become

and the worse everything smells

Close-to
       beneath the choking yellow damp
             the tough evergreen
      of the hedges
      goes shapelessly black as if these were the door lids
          down to caves

so different from Wordsworth's golden mist
         that after the roaring in the wind all night
         shone on the wet green and on the hares
           running so fast the mist flowed after them
    where a slow man went
           bent
            barefoot through the marshpools
            of the rural nineteenth century

he who was so   glad
         of everything
     despite the paltry harvest of fresh leeches
          with their accurate anesthetic
       which could be sold to healers
          for his livelihood

But here against the boiling sound of cars
near the airport off route 10

no one's on foot

     as if it were a kind of shame
         to go thus unprotected
nobody walks

footsteps at the motel clatter quickly
        up the thin but weirdly heavy stairs
     made of dried curds of vomit and soft drink
          cemented into slabs and edged with metal
       then hung on curling sleazy wrought iron rods

to halt is fearful

nobody stops to see the moon

nobody pleasantly ambles forth
        into the inland empire   chest high   arms free
     to take this air of ash and cadmium and air force base perchlorate
        into the flesh

nobody notices the noise of waters   without half-hearing
             in the canyons
     the unwettable ravel of delayed-burn chaparral
        begin its slide

Lyke as the hart desireth the water-brooks
     the psalmist wrote
         through the clear cadences of Miles Coverdale
So longeth my soul after thee

another partition placed upon
         the natural world   that put its faith
   in longing   in an animal
     the hart with branching horns   whose instinct draws
     him to the pure low brook
        no caravan or market dung has muddied
   nor crag upstream comes into nor bubbling
     mineral or gas   or swollen corpse or even transparent
   horde of genetically changing mayflies
          to lay their eggs upon the still unsullied
   emptiness of the quick aerobic water

O God invisible as air

My tears have been my meat

                       sweet
            because no noxious thing runs with them   only
fragrant naïveté of the reflective midday   when
        bank herb and wood flower and water from the pool
          can best be gathered
                         also the knowledge
      that these gifts are tenuous and that the harp
      and the mouth
            might soon be strange to play

for this was the tongue of English images
        wet with northern rainfall   and devotion   inland ocean
          freshet   and frequent rainbow and cold spring and not
    a place made mineral by thirst and harsh tectonics and
        in one prophet's warning

          torrential landforms

resembling Israel or Crete   or dangerous like most
    sweet-looking blue-rose sunsets at the sea's edge

             (where   yes   *One deep calleth another*

beneath Laguna and Long Beach

California Sorrow

MOUNTAIN VIEW

Mountains did   look in
    the windows of the thin aluminum room
    over loud tar paper roofs

    We could see how
peaks
covered with lime or snow
backed away
    a little wounded
from their literal distance

Bruce all night
abject
    the moonlight chafed the bed

his eyes also hot
watching me
burning his will into act so he could keep
lifting me waking me

    (with their strange bodies

from the shallows of half-sleep
in which there was no ground
to anchor in

    (men move in another world

    How could I
shoulder back
the shoulders of his yearning
where he lay
    clothed

atop the sheets his
desire changed by devotion
but still desire awake alive
flooding the atmosphere

     (everything he had to give
     was given
     and I did not want it

————

always in the ear
like a drone instrument

the highway

CLAREMONT RAGA

Languorous landscape
                    homogeneous compact
          lizards making ladder steps
          on fine-combed gravel
          Canary Island date palms
          white stucco and red tile

where for two years an almost forgotten woman posed
in passing
               she had almost
          forgotten   herself
                    blurred there by devotion

outside the arch of a collegiate hacienda

          set against the mountains

her straw mesh hat dimpled
over the shining face

               (Lean forward, let your eyes glaze
               over what falls from them

her past pensive   invisible
but implied
          all she had been deprived of
          all she would live alongside of
                              halfway around the world
                    the moment in the rose garden
                    the fountain empty of everything but light
                    the roses nodding with a minatory loveliness
          toward the monkish traveler

———

Here one could hear the lisp and wrinkle of water
in a dozen working fountains   down colonnades of palm and
eucalyptus in their peculiar tatters above the perfect
moist lawns of small bladed Bermuda grass

What is it makes the brimming of detail
in a moment of amiable privilege
that was not hers
so full of wistfulness

Who knew how hard
her disappointment was
          to wait upon this genius
          of postponement

————

Everywhere the poems open
Ash-Wednesday, the Quartets

misgivings jar his certainties
          about the ways

neither from nor toward

made to carry
a merely *positive* glory
the moment by definition frail

infirm

all the past ruined

the way up

the way down

the present pierced

The sound of water so perfected it
starts to rasp in front of these
            arrested lovers

lady of silences
                    once the hyacinth girl

poet of desuetude
                    whose decaying hope

and holy calling rest upon
the great note in the hymn toward which long varying
and allusion
                    waver

                        as the long neck of the sitar
            seems to bend on the player's heart
            when in bliss he slides the string against it

meanwhile the myriad blood-warming
rhythms and the nine emotions
collide and hover
collide and brood   so that
the note that is never heard

called *anahad nad*
                        the one un-
                    manifested and

                    unstruck

                    comes closer
                    and more clear

AT THE IN AND OUT

While in Southern California
inadvertently working on a suntan
and having had occasion to smile against the light
from a small boat returning to Corona del Mar

Eliot wished to ride with Emily Hale
east in her little roadster
across a scrubby desert
to a hamburger place called the In and Out
that became famous with the poets

Kenneth Koch came there with Marianne Moore
though she brought along
her mother's own tiny picnic
which Kenneth refused to eat
the gooseberries at least seemed to him
too much like muscles
flayed

Daryl Hine who wrote his epic autobiography
called *In and Out* in anapestic trimeters
in open allusion to the food stop's
triangular prism of whitewashed walls
with neon pouring over the drive-through

a mere cookstove above a sewer

        (emblem of an aberrant desire

on a slanted wedge-slice of concrete
                                        where later
steep packed ramps would meet
above a highway

Dickinson came here
(she liked to kneel on sand) and Henry Thoreau
(who liked to scavenge)

James brought a better appetite for beef
than almost anyone   though Tom
        despite the squeamishness
found meat and salt and plumes of fire
licking at the fat
invigorating
for his purgatorial masques

        Emily Hale brings a little rough white paper napkin
        with an almost invisible waffle weave
        and very little absorptive draw
        to the corner of his mouth to take off mustard

The scene feels a little like a Buñuel film
or a Fellini
                the same
crowd going to all the dives and waysides
with all the attendant rustle
                        getting in and out of vehicles
taking their seats   obtaining refreshment *I think*
I'll have a cassis with vermouth says Gary Snyder

the same crowd   raking up
the threads of old conversations
Jerzy Kosinski comes in
lugging a car battery he has stolen

Everyone looking for a new life in the desert

in this twittering world where

they seem to tread on faces   *on*

convulsive thighs and knees

behind these   all the other thieves
cons liars collaborators stagger
       Dantesque   thirsty
              Katherine Mansfield who took from Chekhov
              Gertrude Stein who turned a blind eye
              anti-Semites
                   awed by Eliot
                       Pound who thinks he sees
                  the voice above the urn at Akr Çaar
                  writhing with forgiveness

Also come those who all their lives were cold
       the little Match Girl and Charlotte Mew and Kafka
             hoping to feel   before night drains the sand
       the sinking wick of warmth

Though not entirely sure
who all the others in this circle of the desert
are
       everyone
seems to get along
except Ottolene Morrell
with the shadow in her mouth
who orders a Double Double Animal Style
complaining that *That awful American woman Miss Hale*
was too *like a sergeant major*
probably because she is neatly dressed
and stands quite tall

———————

The images falter and disperse
into the years of separation
       resembling suffering
       with a mouth in O

Hale and Eliot like cutouts
of giraffes
against the dusty sunset

his fluid overcoat and *good walk*
her rakish Robin Hood with the sharp feather

his parted hair
her hair marcelled

his stare
her flowers

VIGIL

There was a door
And I could not open it. I could not touch the handle.
—Edward, in *The Cocktail Party*

1933

When Emily Hale returned to Scripps after Tom's American tour
she carried back the elkhound and the ring he had given her

                                   oddly elegant

accoutrements says his biographer
            as if with these archaic gifts he would lift her out
onto the long unreal imitation of an espousal as on a temporary stage
he had led her to   bearing tokens of a vow
as of two persons whose very bodies suffered
when apart   even if
their bodies never married

although the image
                 broods
      above that threshold

But standing ever ready in her slimness and grace
generous flexible clever
able to project into any theater
and seeming to grow stronger with her years
       although her relatives' Boston
       nicety made it unthinkable
       she should act *professionally*   the while
her academic posts became more meagre and short-lived

she kept her dignified posture
          a cross between
          dorm mother and informal muse
toward the young women in her care   .

as Sappho may have toward the girls in her academy
                    to whom
          preparing for their inevitable destinies as females in Greek society
one scholar says
          her yearning lyrics were meant to provide a kind of emotional
          instruction
                    leading to marriage

and then
          not even academic
                    the posts were more procedural

until after 1948 when Vivienne died

and Emily had believed the fourth waiting over

          the first having been his retreat to England
                    and marriage
          the second the vow of celibacy announced
          in 1928   the third the period
                    entre deux guerres
                    when sin flickered over the landscapes
                              of unreal happiness
                                        the Eumenides looking on
          the fourth   hot penitence for the death
                    of the long imprisoned ghost

after these four   and the terrible
          rejection through another decade when he

          hid from her

Eliot in 1957 married his buxom secretary

and Emily's fine heart broke

and Eliot lived out his time in self-indulgence and
brusque shame   toying
catlike with leftover words

FEMININE CASE

UC IRVINE

In the shells of the corridors
abandoned for the summer
to the language labs

we begin each day

      just after the long rolls of purple smog
      sink toward LA

to talk talk talk
our mouths exhausted and made fearless
by the German

            Never the *best* language student
never ready with the idiom
or the illogical
gender
      three to choose from   that make my thought
      a nightmare of digression from
      the dance I might have set to s-v-o

      verb in the middle like a fulcrum

(because I don't know how to sex the nouns)

therefore I beat them
beat it
down to a suffixed thing
      movement hardened
      into a female key
      —*heit*

                —keit

                     —schaft

                          —ung

worse than the
scientific tongue with its
helpless aversion to the verb
the nouns like chalk
in the drink that
                even in English
makes the water
slurry

       —detriment (once able as *deterere*
           to wear away
                     impair
           something
           standing free)
turns the thing freestanding to a
concept
           more porous than its etymology

       —transposition (one can still almost
see the hand lifting
the thing to place it   pose it
                      further off
where it disappears and disappears
           before us)

       —adventitiousness (from *venire* to arrive, but now
           stumbling in on accident

it cannot move)

          Or sometimes the verb with the false limbs will
fall down its own stairs from *fenestra* window
pushed out the window as *defenestrate*
into *defenestration*   accumulation of the acts of
      push or *being pushed*

out into the air
          above the moat

every predicate
clubbed to dirt   each substantive
feminine and spiny
with abstraction   so:

      rather than admire or fear
the active way she
               drapes each answer
     in its fluent cloth
I make up a patch of German
              that masks an answer

      Antwort-

with disguise

      tarnung s.f.

      (Then was this <u>her</u> story

I try to say she seemed to sleepwalk through
her slippery
indefinite being
     but make it
         Unzuverlässigkeits- (shiftiness's)
            —(dreaminess) *verträumtheit s.f.*
      whose hidden verbs for leave and dream are shorn
        of their futurity
               all their force a block
          without an exit

     (or accidental map
        of her wrong turning

When she looks backward   that
road she had come

grows blurry   hence
       Rückblicksverzerrung (distortion of recall)

to which she might respond with
       Abscheugeziertheit (an affectation of distaste)

      (or one dream more
        agley in language

Backward to her innocence
       she builds herself again
    but my noun could never
follow her there on the springs
        of predication
for she has to crawl beneath the shell's weight
sweating against the slick
    nacre of an airless dome
to pull the weary *thing*
      the
      [noun-ability] to resume
original shape
      Rückbildungs- (reverse-self-shaping)
       —*fähigkeit s.f.* (facility)

Thought crept off to states
      instead of sentences

dream-shiftingness, torn-off back-looking, self-regeneratability, artificial hatred

little countries of abstraction

and the nouns I was avoiding
shining over them like airy lanterns
    of the truth
      cloth and *road* and *answer*
       nausea and *youth*
        stunned
     into unspeaking
      pieces that would never move

their flickering dodgy broken-reeded
            serpentine uncertain

footing

        encumbered

        cobwebbed

                rooted

like the women in Ovid

            each of their shadows thrown all one way
            into the room
                        where all the words pile up
            and the time of day

                    unchanging

With a Shifting Key

—by Paul Celan

With a shifting key
you open the house in which
a smothered secret snows.
In the same way blood wells up and spills
from your eye or mouth or ear,
your key dissolves.

If your key changes, so will the word
that might move in among the flakes.
But like the wind as it cuffs you out,
the snow ices tight to your word.

Brand

The snow ices tight to your word
—Paul Celan

Gale
          gorge wind
with narrow water and
narrowing of her soul that enters it
to be released to what
she cannot now resist

          eternity

glistening and spreading
          when it leaves the fjord
          that grinds her

          (The past with all its laughter thinned
          in the rude air

Here rose the fugue of poverty

          a husband's voice like crags
                    shearing
          self-denial to make her heart beat fast
          hunger's final seasons when disease
                    is easy at its coming in and
                              delirium
          brings back the image of the child
                    who could not breathe in zero

Here are his clothes
Brand has pronounced
she must all give away

Brand now everywhere in her soul
even at the threshold where she hides
in her heart
        where he can plainly see

          Alf's shirt

               with the idea of saving it

Brand draws
her loudly and convulsively
to more denial   even to harm

Harm the talisman
       the avalanche
       that keeps him lean and free

The Poems I Am Not Writing

"Vielleicht daß ich durch schwere Berge gehe / in harten Adern"

Why should I believe there are poems waiting for me which I am not writing?
Because I miss them, these shadows like birds dying of cold on the branches,
their life diminished as I move closer to them. I frighten them with my
nearness. Everything I say in prose, with its links, its clauses, its causal
flourishes; its reservations and chatter of afterthought; everything with prose's
anecdote and self-observation and preening that is like the shiver of a body
brushing back its hair before going into the room, dispels the poem.
Explanations and the appeal to authority tear down the modesty of poetry. Its
near invisibility. Its perfected impermanence. A scat of wind through a tall
fir that knocks off all its caught-up snow and causes the branch to spring
about . . . but in smaller, evaporated language that brings no attention to itself
because it belongs to something greater—perhaps the greater "Whisper of
running streams, and winter lightning" Eliot wrote of as part of his own world
of debased, involuntary phantoms.

Prose tries to be only itself and while it does so, it is not poetry. Yet there are all too many experiences that come back only as themselves. Not a shred of divination in them, only a thin and grimacing reality. Here was one. We were walking near the Arkansas River, although the river's water was now running only at the sides of sandy-blond flats that looked like a beach in the middle of the wet. We were visiting in Tulsa. We walked along the high ridge between the street called Riverside Drive and that low sluggish thing where a blue open river *used* to run up, almost to the level where my father had taken us out, with the handsome, fidgety collie. On the other bank were the colossal white drums containing natural gas. This dog with his lovely axe-swift bark was probably also bothered by the faintly stinking trough that used to be a river. This reminded me of the most mysterious and horrible thing about my grandmother's house. It had a wheel made all of metal, fixed flat on the concrete floor of her basement, like a wheel that you used to seal a door in a ship. It was near a gradual dip in the floor that went down to a dark drain with an open metal grid on top of it. Whenever she did her laundry, water that smelled like the river backed up into her house, and she would have to release it again. "That is sewage," she said, drawing up her top lip; I think she may have said "sewerage," but I clung to the nastiness of the word *sewage*. The sewage water, mixed with suds, would come up only to a certain line on the concrete floor, and then take itself back down when she stooped over and tugged against the sewage wheel. The sewage smell kept to the basement, strongest when you first opened the door to go down, but I think it stayed in your nose. This was also the house where, when you touched the door of the refrigerator and the light switch at the same time, an attentive ripple would come up through your fingers and skim along your arm—as if you were being *watched* by the electricity, and a little scolded.

We were always, more generally, being a little scolded. Perhaps I never felt the difference between the world of children and *their* world more than I did here. It was cold, but with no snow, no moisture, just a drying-out and breaking-down cold. We were always out in it longer than we wanted because the ground was brown and hard and, when seen from indoors, benign. So we were allowed—in retrospect it is clear we were expected—to play outdoors hour upon hour in the chilly leaves below the evenly allocated, faintly stinking, windless, bony dusk.

That is what I mean. "Windless, bony dusk" is rather good, but in *prose* it is just too pleased with itself. A poem I am not writing yet might chasten it.

Notes from earlier decades. Traces of poems vanishing like straw in mud. Unabsorbed events. Grimaces of reality that I also fear because they block the lightning of forgetfulness. Even the dreams disturbing and complex. Regret, resentment, yearning, apprehension in both senses, suffering, and desire—but always stopped in gargoyle postures. Those scraps of loosened handwriting, jotted down late at night, confessions stiffened by self-consciousness and peculiar longings and equally peculiar vanities and the urge to destroy and the urge to shine and (therefore) memories with the unnaturally strong shoulders of fiction: All of this avid pinning-down proved how great was the rift between the surges of will and the power of intuition.

Lost Poems Like

those streets down which
sun never falls

Above which
stories cloud up
with a god onlooking
twisting about the sky
The poems to burn through into code

like an opera in silver

When death begins
the muscles under the teeth and jaw
disintegrate down to the chest
That is death   that
the flame goes on rotting
in the windless bony dusk

The last phrase is no longer a bas relief standing out, polished, "rather good,"
above the smooth ground. It is desolate. Anger watches it. Fear drains it. Spirit
is already gone from it. It is an afterwards, not an apex. Nothing follows.

When I turned fifty I couldn't read in a book at night. It turned out I couldn't see. I had to get my first pair of glasses—not just to be able to read, but also to see at a distance. I was given trifocal lenses, with different prescriptions in the upper and lower thirds, and no prescription in the middle (this was where I could see people walking toward me and the license tag of a car that was pulling away; but where it counted, the codes of shape were stormy). With the glasses on, I couldn't walk straight or change levels, couldn't find the right focal depth, which was too tiny to lock in on quickly. I fell down stairs. I tripped. I was falling out of coincidence with myself. I was blurred in space as things in space were blurred in front of me. I was far away from where I thought I was. My hands weren't useful. My mind wandered. I disliked to read: I dithered. I would get distracted by money worry, and would work for a time each day with a small solar powered calculator.

Chores grew heavier, also doing my job, which was a never-ending humiliation. The surer I became about the mystery of words in time, the more intricate the disdain of the professionals around me. This was a world in which there was a constant encouragement to promote oneself, to mention every little mention of oneself. To be your own entrepreneur. Deadly to art. I tried not to play, but did just a little—enough so that I neither made a good showing among *them* nor kept my heart pure. Caving in "just a little" is the hateful form of humiliation, for one is driven by fear of going under, by doing nothing. This anxiety doesn't end with a small cowardice. It is a world based on *worry*, because they themselves are always heartily, greedily worrying, scratching the sand of their little plots of earth.

Is this behavior so harmless? Artists in the middle ages knew that the world of functionaries in the chicken yard, distracted by little lies, ran parallel to a world of gruesomeness. The able knight was served by the gnomes of hell, the innocent child by leering familiars who turned into puppets of fang and gore as soon as they turned their faces away. In my dreams, I was like the disintegrating ones, teeth exposed to the chin and a premonition of my end told by the pain that reached across my chest. I couldn't cry out. I couldn't be kind. The jaw was clamped. This was what I would die of, but would I be struck? would it happen among others?

How many women think of themselves as tiny mechanical dancers on a music box. "Failures of nerve and energy are not permitted," I wrote; "that's what it means to be an object." And a jolly crust is a kind of thing-making, too, a forcing by the world, to which one dare not show the shrinking and weeping within. Does prolonged distress really humanize the soul? Hardens it, rather; even the raw spots that never heal grow hard. Shyness is not the recoil of something tender but the locking away of something already ruined. It comes to the surface in childhood. No, not the surface. It presents itself like a tiny ledge on a sheer mountain. This is impossible to step off from because beyond the ledge there is only silence and the long drop. Speech seems irrelevant— can you *speak* your way out of the punishment of gravity? I looked at those other figures, roped safely to crags of dark matter; who could speak, in full sentences, in public, marshaling example and parallel, followed by foreclosed countercase, speeding toward the warm updraft of conclusion. Still, rhetoric must first presume that others listen and attend to you, otherwise it is mad.

Attend LAT *tendere* to stretch *attendere* to stretch toward: to take care of to look after accompany be present (at) await. Without attention, nothing can proceed. Thought stops in its tracks, or rants. Thought drags itself *inside*. One becomes haunted by muteness, among mute things.

Stevens thought that things, which were once human, had lost their former power to conceal themselves. But if we imagine things as having once been persons, wouldn't they retain at least the shape of their once symbolic hulls, however little they could now hide within them? Isn't the material world fundamentally a kind of vulnerable or inept concealment?— A fly apparently buzzing in place within the web, but in a shell the spider has siphoned the strength out of, moved now only by the wind. . . . The reflection of a stone granary in the mere. . . . Freckled leopard apricots. . . . Grace that has been frozen—a bicycle frame like an antelope; a submerged jar; a shoe made of willow. At the edge of a hot field, a cow shed and chicken coop; beyond these, in a forest of hard blue, the "pierced iron shadow of the cedars" (Marianne Moore). Close around them, against the male sun and the cool female forest, the stretch of ground somebody has mowed despite the desolation of these frames with their sagging silvery boards. The coop. The shed. Who abandoned them and yet comes back to mow? Don't ask realistic questions. Patience, soon you will sleep too.

Sometimes the world of things has something to say. Randall Jarrell wrote that stream water made a sound that was like a spoon or glass breathing.

Now we are awake together just after I have come in to get her from her nap. I have had my hair cut. My daughter looks over my head for the clue to the newness. *As if to find the strings that pull me.* Her attention is radiant. Attention: careful observing thoughtful consideration of others readiness to respond observant care. Agility. Transparency. We are in a half-darkened room together, with a bit of brick and sky visible out the window and a small rough white cloud scooting by. It is a moment. It promises to move, quickly, away from itself, out into time. To stop it spilling over, we understand that we would be happy to *stay*, as we are, leaning with the side of the crib between us, both standing, making small shifts. We know that everything is before us, including the steepening light and the "haar trees" (willows) bobbing a little. All the years we have spent together since then—all those moments of nearness without possession—were before us. But they no longer include that moment.

Mania might spur it on again, the work of the poem, as it did with Pound, wanton, clumsy. As a permission, however, not a working method. For it is also weak to be a storm, self-obscuring. How can temper release poems, or lead one down to them again? Perhaps it never could. For it is also weak to be a storm, self-obscuring. If poems are given to a sufferer, they may be epiphenomena, like steam from the pavement after a cloudburst. Real, but tenuous.

If the only way to live
were to be cold
moss and leaf mold
up in the box elder
water coating me
with a steady weeping
through which nothing
warm blooded
breathing fog
would ever pass again

or to be feral
in cold

would I choose this
and go on
      or
      or

Poems have entered my being only after a stupor of watching, running my eye down the flaking seams. Except that now the mineral is hard and serious, at the level at which I must mine, and little moisture reaches its refreshment down. The stone has anchored itself together against anything that wants to grow. Perhaps I am like the hard vein that moves through Rilke's equally rigid mountain? Hardness clamped within hardness. No breath of distance. This sense that the light, the gift, the water has been withdrawn might still lead to poetry, I suppose—hypothetically conceived. Job today, not Job as he knew himself yesterday. But Job was not Job in that yesterday life. He is Job only where he is now, his terrain of deprivation the dense impacted slab of mountain, a waste crag far above the tree line, which irritates and sets off the self-involved, hugely suffering, heroic will—and this is out of my reach. (My place is really more like a parking lot.) No Job yesterday either, of course, with the hard rock pouring out, for me, a stream of oil. A daughter with her soft breathing close to my face and a sense of grace like dew collecting everywhere and making everything lucid. No. Only cars trolling for a parking place and acres of brand names. *Das Herstellbare:* the jumble of gadgets and skills that can be brought-forward-and-placed-before the multitude. The eager grinning of that multitude. The calculator whirring.

Bromide. A dead spa in Oklahoma. I was standing on the running board of a car holding around the post between the front and back windows. It was summer. The people in the car were all my relatives. Grandpa was driving; next to him were the small pair who made fires to keep warm even in summer, Uncle Gerald and his wife Nona, who was part Blackfoot. In the back my mother and father and Percy, who was asleep, then barking, sat next to someone I don't remember. I watched the baby on my mother's lap move her eyes without moving her head. We were driving home from the empty town one of the relatives had built, which was entirely red. Pieces of red stone had also been stuck sideways into the red buildings like parts of saucers. All the panes of glass were yellow with a hard fur of dust that seemed to be growing there.

There was a red fountain, empty, bigger than two cars. I lay down in it and saw nothing but the red sides and the hot blue sky. Everything was dry. Mother put down a quilt on the limited shadow of a tree with a big trunk and no leaves, and we had a thirsty picnic. On the way back I was *very* hot on the outside of the slowly moving car. We came to a place that hadn't been there on the way, where the dry orange road went down into a pool. You could see a bank of dark leaves, partly wet, on the other side of the flooded place, where the rest of the orange road pulled up against the hill. Grandpa stopped and then coasted down. His fingers moved about on the steering wheel. We could *smell* the road going into the water the way you can smell a candle going out. I planted my feet on the running board. The water came over the rubber grids. Do you remember, I asked my mother, how the water came up to my *knees!* When was that, she said. When we were at Bromide with Nona and Gerald and Grandpa and Percy and I lay down in the fountain. Yes I remember, she said, but Nona wasn't there.

We didn't have Percy yet, she said. That was when you were four. And the water was so black, I said, and the sun was in a big circle around us but then the water got dark black again and it was a four-door Packard. Oh darling, she said, you've never been in that car; that was in the album. We'd never have let you do that, anyway, if the road had been flooded.

Memories, word-images like jumps of flame. *Irrlichter.* As if they were things whose life-sparks had become wayward, they coast about our world like particles who have lost the others. How does one remember what was never there?

But the dreams were there.

The words that were over the dreams were there.

I read the dictionary, the record of resemblances, a book that like a drug
releases again the half-heard and the half-understood from the

           the edge   the edge
           where where where

you'd forgotten them. Better still, it puts you at the crossing

           from a time long before   when
           the past of other tongues
                 poured
                       along the present

I discover that a word I thought of as a green liqueur popular in the forties is
also a cloth full of holes (with the seeds of war mistakenly mixed in).
Grenadine FR dim. of *grenade*, pomegranate (in turn from LAT *pomum* apple
granatum stocked with seeds); from being spotted with grains (grain LAT
granus): a thin loosely woven cloth of cotton silk or rayon used for blouses
curtains. What had been dense is charged with a loosening light. The charge
of sources. The action of apt definition. Energy loose and running just below
the surface. A blouse of sheer grenadine. Ash with its wingèd fruit. Brogue a
bond or grip on the tongue. Light pictures. Photographs, which are not images
of living beings but of the light that once shone through them. Lintel, the
timber that binds a doorway at the head or foot or the threshold stepped across
or through. Scrape to make a trench or grave. A grave being scratched out, a
love being frozen. Leaves scrape on the lintel under an icy light. Light turns
the flakes of snow to bits of mica, streams of shadow rising from the radiator
like thin throngs of microscopic creatures or the minute reticulation (net-
work) of high wind on open water.

Open water, which long remembers nothing, neither wind nor wake
        Nemerov wrote

Wake ON *vök* a hole in the ice track left in water by a passing ship the ghost of
something that has passed by. Words as ghosts of all who used them but are
passed away. Haunt OFR *v.t.* to frequent resort to bother pervade visit as a ghost
n. (1) that place lair feeding place (2) also *hant* a ghost. The lesson of Kafka's
burrow: when you're in it (as you are *in* the present moment), you're afraid of
losing it. In fact, with its walls about you, you must see it as already lost.
No lintel.
No hearth.
No haunt.
No time.
No home.

A city truck just went by, pulling, on a flatbed trailer, a small ochre-yellow bulldozer with the brand VERMEER in black block letters shining in significance against the dirt.

Scattersite

Rose of paper

lattice of leafbranch
    woodsy

            coated with sun
fennel ash

wheelrut deepening
    mud turn
    sequin
one quick
    roadway eddy

second growth
lost things
    lost growth
    second things

eddy sequin   slide ground

Bright gift
    silk wit   lining
oil of orange
    bicolor with
      the sleeve

Waft hoard   lift
    life
        wing

        rise   intake

    tongueless light

uncover sky

Facing North

Late Householder, Early Pilgrim Phase

The self is not an object but an act,
an old friend wrote with a sense of the border loosened
into fear, and time that staggers
with its arm about his shoulder in the leaf drift;
yet the thought became so clear, it grew a written
thought, a thought for writing down, drawn out
across the frame of close antithesis
our tongue at once permits and, well, enjoys
while making thought so modestly *more* clear
than it needs to be that truth is piqued
instead of broadened—as the frame we use,
the not wholly mindless now but all too natural
medium of the blank-verse line makes thought
that wanted to be aimless, full of aim,
and the tight shoulders of the slacks and stresses
stay strangely hard and arbitrary
although they may shiver a little when intuition
traces out a line as through humid woods,
which stones emerging along the way like faces
make sharper and more conscious as the words flex
and limber up iambically (*not x but y*
fits well here, too), their shift a kind of
anemone whose tissue flutters in the steady current,
combing water of its nutrients.

        Not thing but will, not with but toward,
        not chair but ledge, not sum but subtrahend:
        how easily the grammar bosses us to the wall,
        not me but you, not surge but drag,
        I'd wish to surge but always feel the drag
        that kept myself from jumping off the ledge
        into a circle whose circumference

you couldn't stand in the center of
and I'd wish I liked
the shifting view from nowhere, more.

———

Here I am with the cat on my lap in a room that faces north,
a thin loaf of rooms with a feeling of long shadow in bright day. Here
in the murk
above the desk where several brand-new strands
of a half-hearted trace of spiderweb keep reappearing,
there are those volumes
of the furnished-rental world, novels too dull or strange to steal:
Arrowsmith, Studs Lonigan,
The Late George Apley, flotsam by Dos Passos,
all the faded froth of the fifties book clubs,
Will Durant alongside Hardy's *Tess*
the latter in a fine hand-tooled edition
with watered silk endpapers—but why *Tess,*
with her harsh fate, in pretty leather? These oddments mount up
like a rattling cage
shaped to an absence.

———

The only other time I'd tried to write
surrounded by such brokenness,
there were two books:
one, by Samuel Butler, I never finished;
and the novel of the emperor Hadrian's love
for the dead ephebe Antinoüs
in whose name and image he raised up beautiful things
all over Asia Minor,
beautiful places, too, where the emperor
as Yourcenar pictures him
walked on the backs of others
through the architectonic emptiness
of memory: It was something he could do.

It filled his time
with fire.

———

That was my leisure reading all one summer
at MacDowell where, when not wandering in the shadow
of Monadnock, I was trying to decode the friendly nervous nonsense
of John Ashbery's "Houseboat Days"
in a cottage where for a while each morning
the sun shone directly down a huge stone chimney
on two demonic andirons with carved eyeholes
blankly attentive
to crickets moving
their sandy legs over the spent ash,
                              " . . . and you
don't see until it's all over how little
there was to learn . . ."

———

       Only when smoke
       from their dinners
       has died down
       and the dishes are removed
       may a pilgrim approach the
       human habitations
       to beg her meal
       untouchable
       on the other side of life

———

Good heavens . . . there I am the previous winter
north of Chicago, north also
of the little city-center candy blocks
of the eastern seaboard,
wandering in Montreal
through a darkening isolation, doubly disloyal,
my French not very good and perhaps a shade

taller than the man I went there with.
He did not like to give or hear endearments.
His French was excellent. The first night drunkenness
carried us off so quickly
it was as if we had left something behind, in that other life,
and without it
the moment wouldn't come into a shape.
A horrible week-end.
I kept thanking him,
an awful sense of wrong making me abject,
"Thank you for our time together"
(by which I meant
to ask myself,
why had I done this?)
and he made an invisible bow
in French,
"Mais c'est á moi." It made me cringe
to think how obvious
abjection is, to think
how Proust thought of Marcel
thinking of his beloved almost as a doll
he had been molding,
"the docile body which he had pressed
tightly in his arms and explored
with his fingers . . ." (The artist's doll . . .)
In the museums, I leaned forward to the tiny paintings
which he said not to touch.

––––––––

No, the self can't mend, it can only want
and pretend not to want,
aloof, disheartened. Here it is,
breaking things all over again
trying to speak of things all over again,
trying to hull them

the wood asters
the tree with the strange leathery leaves,
the smokebush, the beautyberry

caught at dusk in the crinkled leaf veil
of the high thin trees
with the few last flecks of day's white
shimmering high above (was I under water?) . . .

all the reality whose exactness
has lost its dignity

and the desk where the words for this
move on a piece of paper
       facing north.

First Passion

Running   there I am   at fourteen
          I have been scolded
by my father for something I hadn't done
or hadn't not done   who knows   the dishes   nothing
          serious like my smoking
                    or ineptness with people and bad
          choices

                    It was *unjust*
and the almost irrelevant injustice grew so pure and tiny
          in its atmosphere of truth
                    which rose like sky
that I fell in love with it and it cut into me

          loosening the first tears

          (though these were not what frightened me at night

Then the griefs came loose   beginning to run   I was
          fourteen and
                    wailed around the blocks
                              more times than once
          my chest   straining against the sobs
                    in their delightful echoing
          back from the streets that suddenly were empty

                    everyone having
                    inched backward from the windows
                              into the parts of rooms that are never chosen
                    the side of the stairs   the door
                              to the water heater
                                        where they watched
          me amazed at this sourceless melodious grief
                    eager to return to the normal dithering watchful
                              golden gossip   of the afternoon

Privilege

A bit of progress   in the writing under weigh
folders safe for the night
                    over their pilot lights

All this   smooth background
               under the westward striking sky

makes emotion   kind

where focal distance opens out
                    and one sees the world
                                        a little

Glints jostled by their trembling

tiny oval-bladed leaves
               bend the sun
                              a treble refraction
really   through
               eyelashes   trifocal
                    graduated lenses
               leaves of the willow oak

a moiré of prisms
                              at just the angle so the whole
thing tenses
                    in huge repeating aureoles of brilliance
                    palely rainbowed   at each ray's end
                              like folk art

I thought
                    (through the sunwarmed funnel of wine
                         at day's end

we were all

leaves   wishes   lightforms   air

harmless enough

Then through the leaf fan comes
the tiny remembered bowl
of a northern lake
               the wavelets sliced
               by strips of light

       brown white brown white

white thickening to gold   brown falling into black
as the sun
           cools above its precipice

This was where   one summer   too many of the family
in a froth of candor before each other
upbraided my father for his flaws
               not looking
about them at what he had made for us

driving himself
                   by who knew how much
         shortening his life and hardening his outlook

so we would have a little dock by the spangle of water
and could sleep summers under fresh leaves

         though in time he had to sell it

Whenever the year turns cool I smell it   the reunion
        when I did not come to his defense
        against the crude publicity of their
            apparently reluctantly outspoken
        disrespect

loud badge of their new selving
which he took in without objection

Although his temperament is
as it always was   humorous   impatient   disappointed
quiet has
continued to fall
from his bruises

white brown white brown
waves thin as pens
that copy then
cross out

Hardly harmless

all the privileged children he has raised
all of his children's babies and their children's
with perfectly formed
small feet and able toes
never had to plunge daylong
into the rolls of sparkling filth
glinting with tin
in the billow raised by the up-
scooping plow
of the earthtreading dredge
in a garbage marsh

where in a crowd of flies loud as Beelzebub
masked with rags
the shoeless Indonesian five-year-olds
clamber up and down the spongy surface
inches from the treads
to pluck out deftly with their homemade sticks
the bits of newly reemerging serrated broken junk
someone will pay them two cents per heavy bushel
to recycle

But if they did not ruin their days   revolving time
          inside a turning drum of hours
                         sifting through
            already sifted-through dripping debris

who would give us our   wasteful

            wistful hours
                          of self-righteous
     need

Sale

Older now, he is among us in diminished form,
clothes sagging, hat large on the fine head

He likes the largest stores   acres of socks and tuna   where
       high girders look down on him also   who
         pushes his cart and leans on it a little
. . . something sacramental about the belittling
perspective   something
      heroic about the high shadows in the niches
       of the corrugated roof
           beneath which
         under spotlights that don't spread far
he moves with the people who comb through
the aisles   pulling down unwieldy
     batches of single things   to last them through
     cold time
       that can't be trusted

There he is at the far end of an avenue
           of obelisks of paper
head cunningly mobile like a bird's   eyes quick like one
     beading on flecks that might be the
       morsels that it needs
       or on grains   or seeds

At this its faltering morse of chirrups   but no long address
     only
       the same few wordchains

    at my feet
      water water water

    millet beak millet crack millet

air down danger aieeeeeee

But in their multitudes   horrific
      squeals
          blue golden green their throats and breasts
    all with the herringbone
        wingcaps that grind like blades
          of a thousand ceiling fans in a
          flaming house

After the teak forests were hewn down   plagues
    of parakeets rippled down on the crops
        themselves a crop   digesting
      menacing
        no longer charming and
      observable

but like any swarm or heap or tumulus or
    housing project or array of products or uncountable mass
      of faces even rich ones

      repellant

You can almost see them in his mind
    my father's wordchains as they click against each other

        rapidly succeeding in his mind

I've got to get there   *got to*
    bank today   *to get to sleep*   *to shave*

    got not to wait
      a second longer for what I've earned
    my whole life through the right to want
      without excuse

and he thinks the people at the other end are
    idiots   or

when things are going well
just helpless
or when they know a little fact
that he does not
(that beating flour too fine will mean the gluten
cancels out the baking soda and the rolls
won't rise
well   then   that they are smart
as whips

Eyes almost black behind his glasses   shining
before the freezer cases of brightly packaged
dinners with too much
sodium and fat
rounds of chicken   steaming
like eager faces against the costly frost

he flies up into the highest branches
of the possible air   and then goes still
at everything spread down there   for sale

A Parakeet

There was my father's short sister rushing down the street
with white light flying out her fingerends
from a kitchen towel with which she must have sought
to lure or drive or flutter space down upon
(to calm it

a chartreuse parakeet
upright in grasshopper green against
the thick tip of a tall poplar bare of leaves

One of her children ran after with the birdcage

Nothing tragic closes the anecdote

It never became an anecdote
When I began
to tell it   ask it   to the cousins
did she scold down the parakeet
the grownups at the edges of the hour all seemed
to turn their backs
from the room with the noontime hellish kids' TV show
and her children Joan
and John Paul and Stephen and Bobbie Ann
went blank and jumpy
as they ate their pb and j and drank their milk

as if I hadn't spoken
or were no longer there
as if they had never had a parakeet
as if the creature
near the TV were new
or never missing   or would
only flee the house in some
far future after they'd

              moved away
        while I could not
     not see it in all the time that would pass   then
till now
here   as it stood up like a woodpecker against the bark

green as the green of sun on murky water

as she made her distant warble to the world
        (though she was more used to saying it
          to herself

The aunt is dead
     and the youngest
          female cousin with the bones of a bird

They haven't spoken

       but they know

Mantid

Below the water table
even when the ground seems still

waves
        in frequencies so long the graph bar
        flattens
curve between the colored-taffy strata

Further toward the surface   in my tiny flat
           with the high ceiling   a stretch
       goes through the things
               breathing
         molecules of moisture
       with a tinny crackle
         into the chair leg   the floor

Even windless
       nights are apt to stripe the asphalt with
the faring-forward sizzle of the cars   taking people
fast
       out of the shouting houses
          creating airwaves that gaily
       tighten the clasp of rage
           upon the steering wheel

       and whisper
         the joists of the building

These inferences of motion may have made
something like a small book
       or slew of letters
           slide to the floor
               (an article or pamphlet

for no reason now   except the stacks of things
                had been on edge so long

        (a sheaf of notes
                        near the edge of the shelf
                (a scrolled up magazine   soft with humidity

but none of these
none
        would have fallen
                in the window

From the first vaguely woody
                        vaguely raglike bump
I knew it was something to deal with

        very probably alive

and   despite the want of scurry or flight   that
                its nature was to move

It turns out its nature was to freeze

As close to it as I dared
                        (no way to tell it from the floor
                                except for its being rough
                        like bark
                or very slightly underlighted

        forearms   like serrated sticks
                slow as
        the battens in dead flags
                hung from a pediment

        swung above the long
                oval swab of the abdomen

        significant

a female's

What *drew* her   had she been
                    alerted by the hollow in her
                metathorax to
        the swooping signal of a bat
                    to make her take that strange evasive
                corkscrew dive into
                            my bedroom

and was she now relieved . . .

She made a sound like an old leaf
dragging across cement
her tiny heart-shaped head
like a dull jewel on a hinge
            that during mating would turn toward
                    her smaller partner
            with open jaw

        (even brainless   the male's
                    operative parts
                            still go

    after which the female
            finishes
                the body

Was she now   I wondered
                            sated
                    heavy with egg

or so disoriented by desire   she crawled toward any light
            which might seem like reflection up from water

against whose dancing skin
wings   even the small birds'

beaks
could be detected

Here she came   articulating toward the light

I had stood on the bed
      backing away
            I must have looked cloudy
      my arms like logs

There was no way
          because the creature could not

     push the crumpled water up ahead like the poet's
             apparition of unrejoiced reply
      or *force the underbrush*

         because she could not
fly   because she could not
turn herself
     or change in time
       except down the generations

There was no way
         in this little place with the tall ceiling
   in my state at the time
      in which daydreaming with a black stare

        harrowed

   the furrows of the silence toward
      one distant figure
        on maneuvers
          who had run into a fondness for refusal

        along with all the pause and paradox that
           like a damper pedal
                    pressed
       the long decay of sound   of delicate
           diatonic hum   elapsing
                    through an overcast of near-notes
          into a present ghost . . .

    There was for us   I say   no way
           to end this encounter

      well

Like a Furnace

Voices and music from another house mock the darkness with their sharp self-knowing

      as if hissing sparklers had been tossed into my room

Other evenings the silence is so pronounced no sound of mine can cut through it, and then the lamps seem to drink from the dimness of the molecules.

It is a room in which, overnight, all of the cat's moods rattle about. By morning the rugs are clumped. The crewelwork fabric on the back of the old rocker hangs in longer shreds. Dirt from the potted Norfolk pine peppers the walls. Bad, bad moods. The isolated freaks of an indoor cat who must play through the long wakeful cupboards of the night.

When I open the door to let her into the kitchen, she rolls quickly, luxuriantly, on her back, loudly purring, opening her spiny mouth to mew. The bliss of companionship. Fun with string. Bird watching. She runs at her dish of food.

After fifty, it's harder to see the skin of your knuckles or heels without the help of glasses. You are more wakeful but less agile.

Sometime during the indefinite past the other side of fifty, there was a hair under my chin that I could feel, but not see. I asked my daughter to pluck it. This she did helpfully, efficiently, and I could feel that memorable warm breathing that only comes against the skin of your face when someone who loves you with calm love is looking at you closely, from nearby.

Affection also occasionally overflows the material world. Certain writers seem to meet its hard surfaces with such intuitive tact that these bend and open. Montale, for example. He wrote of a hotel's revolving door that it "moves shiningly upon its four leaves— / One leaf answers another, flashing a message!" He also spoke of souls at a crossing like bottles that could not open themselves. Montale the shining, genius of secondary spirits, who knew how needful it may be to reflect upon the grime that made the silver of appearance sparkle so.

But then there is the world of Homer, in which brutality overwhelms composure and dignity, even if, far from the battle, the horses of Achilles weep silently at the death of Patroclus.

From the brutality of Homer it is little relief to move to the anomie of someone like Beckett, who puts the self in a jar: *all* words, held up in glass, a rivery mania of language, but no chance to change in time. Not even a missed chance.

All the apartment blocks in Dostoevski, the misguided sprawl of Brasília, the crumbling landings of Cabrini Greens: zones poorly built and cracked apart by wretchedness. Crowded emptiness of endless labor. Turbines: Salgado. Scorched earth: Nachtwey. Windows out of which one sees only dead ground and closed horizons and more buildings—and then the random cruelty after.

Yet the apartment blocks in Kieslowski's *Decalogue* rise away from the dour materials to which they seem, superficially, reduced: this clump of 1950s multistory buildings that is the setting for the ten films is the home of surprisingly human beings who radiate the spirit's strength to work against its own weakness, even by caving in. (Well, *another* sort of caving in. The commandments are broken.) There is tragedy and honor and betrayal and mistaken devotion and clever, desperate fallibility and love redemptive, unfolding, being tested—and withstood—inside those prefab concrete rooms into which the always gray light travels only part of the way.

Is my impression accurate?—that the film could not have unfolded in Florida or Des Moines? That it must be Warsaw with its metallic geometries and carefully preserved allegories of ice and destitution? How do the people survive there, where melancholy is so highly evolved: No rain against green things, only rivulets of gray slag. Even in springtime, a temperature only ten degrees above freezing.

But even as I write about such morbid weather, something starts to flame in my heart.

There was a thin layer of wet snow last night, snow-rain falling today through the unpleasantly green-gray overcast now deepening into dusk. The cold has been

        startling   sent over the pools
           of standing water   like messages of
         scorn   these
         first thin
         calluses of ice

Graupel floats in the thickness of some pines near the dump:

            discs of darkness coast near the weeds
               braceleted with froth
                     and over the ankle depth
           of muddy water as if
         from the tentative pressure of hands

                       Wind
      throws down small birds like
        bits of brown felt

Big wet snow starts to fall

It starts amid thunder and, eventually, lightning, the lightning not as surprising because the snow had already made the air so bright. But the thunder is awesome and wrong, creating nausea.

This was the weather of Hewin Castle (by the dark waters of Tarn Wathelyne in Wales) where Arthur's knights fell under enchantment, and of the sixth circle of the *Inferno*, scene of distortions midway between the inhuman and the human, in which Dante's gluttons crowd in, under a storm of filthy hail and black snow, howling like hounds, then trying to shield one flank with another by hopeless squirming. A remnant of human sense makes these bestial changes more sorrowful. These beings howl in the rain like hounds, that is, in Dante's thought, more like things than people.

A friend I don't see much anymore, at the Y, sitting at various places, on the steps going down to the warm pool where the five-year-olds are having a lesson; in the locker room, half-dressed, facing away on a stool, completely still. Her students who had been battered as children. One of them had a Le Creuset mother. "I was a crockery girl myself."

Summer *frisson*. The pleasant dapple from the leaf canopy speaks differently to us than to them (the animals who hide in the shrinking woods, who are driven by the thirst that also drives the insects, to lunge and gnaw). In late summer

> even the days
>> pass away like smoke
>>> grass gray and
>>>> sharp to the touch
>> foil wrappers soft
>>> heat-thinned

In the alley a young girl and boy, she with her legs over his thighs as if on a seesaw too small for her. One finds them here and there in the network of service roads, occasionally veiled by the dust of junk trucks and jalopies playing rap . . . crows poking in each other's gullets for food . . . the beat of coarsening desire which the young learn to look through, almost not hearing the snap of "the silver leash of the will" (Sylvia Plath). The two are still as birds on the edge of a poisoned quarry.

Like Birds

who wait a call
to startle them south
precocious   un-
        protected
early
        marked out
to leave before their time
condensing their will
into detonations of
        tampered pleasure

At the end will
the sawed-off tree

                    as an unpleasant
                    scripture says
bud and put
forth branches
                    dripping pain

Well before it occurred to me that I might become a poet, I moved about
under an horizon of disapproval. Its frown roved

                             like a swollen wave yet
                                    full of splinters

                            light shrieking at each entry
                 paring the present away until

                          until it

                    pounding
                    nerves   too torn to

On the other hand there was the expanse of boredom

               hard to gauge its tape   its contour
                                 the no-thought slick   adherent

Shrieking and boredom.

Much testy, approximate, preoccupied birdsong. Birds strut about after
landing, dark, large, unchallenged. Amid all the chaffing

    another knowledge sinks in
                a spirit glides past her face

            its symptoms
            constant
                    recent grief
            the love that bleeds
            trouble sleeping   the pillow hot
                    the darkness hungry
            exhaustion   the hand
                    too heavy for itself
            thoughts of self-destruction
                    what if she were not   what if
                    the world were to be
                                without that living hand
            inability to eat
                    (the psalmist too
                            let fall
                            his crust

Once, I was in the housekeeper's stage. Now, I am in the pilgrim's—yet it's *she* who is far and I who remain behind, dimmer, diminishing.

> her thinking I am cowardly
> her knowing I
>   postpone   her having to take charge
>   of packing the books
>   before the move
>   before last

> Perhaps I am   near dead
>   I am almost all
>   dreading-to-be-gone
>   as if I were
>   sitting at a bedside where there lies
>   a log half burnt

Without her I am being pressed into the world where, after listless unfolding, bereavement draws in. Sweet, the temptation to give up being human and become fire burning down to the germ of wooden life.

> My bones   too   burn like a furnace

Occasionally, I can still see us, together   yet far away, in the yard of his house
one warm day in autumn.
As usual he stays indoors.
Although it is not something that interests her, she feels kindly about my gardening. She chatters
about what we are doing:
"She planted and snipped and let her daughter dig for a while."
Perhaps she imagines that I am wholly

       absorbed by this raking and stripping and prying open of the ground to hide the bulbs
               the way we believe that any person alert to her work is thinking in one
       single complete preoccupied coherent and unwavering way   and that there is

           delight

      in a skill all pointed upon one task

Perhaps it is only when you have been near someone over time that you know their thinking is a
braid of thoughts all mixed the pertinent and the not and that some thought never stops

          and some
               is never formed

Were we starting an epoch together, artists in arms, his drawings, my poems?

       Would we warm the world
       and make all heads to turn

Or would the feeling of power with no real object except ourselves simply . . .

I imagined it as a path down which our walking would illuminate an intimacy more enormous than anything to which . . . It may have been too much to dedicate myself to, without coming unstuck, un-[ ]ed. Eventually, the image shut, its beginnings dry, its gestures [ ] , all feeling a grimace.

    It turned out my [ ] was not required in the affair. At work was something like Kafka's paradox (about the savior who comes only when no longer necessary).

       I glowed on some dark [ ]
           which no ships passed so near to
               as to need to be [warned?] away

       a light raking the expanse
           no moth was tempted to [burn?] toward

       Among rocks that slid underfoot
           knocking
               in the water   time-smoothed
                  nearly
                 identical
    I [ ] my way

Then, anxious for a large renunciation, I went back to the other. Still glowing a little, but [quelled?] and [   ].

       I go out like
           a cinder

Scraps of paper on which I wrote out the excuses he dictated for me to give over the telephone to the people he worked for.

Heracles brings Alcestis back, veiled, to her husband Admetus, whose life she had saved by giving up her own, asking him now to keep her as a servant. There rises up in Admetus the barely perceptible fear, with this trembling wraith, that he will not be able to obey his wife's dying injunction to be faithful after her death. What if, to change Euripides, Admetus knows the servant is his wife Alcestis, yet refuses to welcome her for fear of seeming to break his pact. How shallow the loneliness of his duty: pitfalls all round, everyone observing.

We sit and observe.

Alcestis remains hidden because she despises Admetus's cowardice but is careful of his self-esteem. Her burden: to have unalterable mastery over her desires despite the unworthiness of their object.

Eventually, when winter was savagely long and seemingly permanent, the fate card fell. I heard her humming with her entire body (she could not yet speak). It was my girl *waiting*

> without oxygen
> knocked about by
> quickly cooling flares

Her breath is warm and comes into my nose. The child is looking closely at me, moving her eyes from one side of my face to the other, gliding with her attention but nevertheless looking with great alertness, and the simplicity of devotion. Does she imagine what my features amount to, what they are *like?* for she is breathing onto my face as if to fix her vision on that other thing, down here in that pool whose upper surface I peer from.

Each sound in the upper world is coldly symbolic. Boom of traffic like surf, children after school spilling across the streets, flashes of relentless music yanking people this way and that, creatures that

> shrill and chirp   following the sun
>
> branch scrapes on branch
>   (what *is* it trying
>   to get in
>
> Limb on limb
> waving down to me
>   *reach up*
>   *shed your skin*
>   *come*
>   *away*

Time calls its segments out: through gears in an old steeple through minutely
eroding crystals on the wrist. Later

            down the eons
            the quartz that measures

            smaller

it will get later each day. Once a given mass of matter is spent
how harness
the ruined molecules stored in caves
from the reactors   Except that

            except that in time

              at last

On the highway, distant trucks make a music like the sea in a cave or wind through a hole.

How fast how far do they drive?

All the way to the longest river.

First they whine along the arable fields, flat as baking sheets; then skirt the bumpy places where the glacier stopped. Lower, as they race down the stump of the Panhandle, the winds pick up speed and ghost towns flicker beneath their veils of orange dust. From the roadside, all this mineral history. Salt flat. Iron spring. Dust bowl.

gypsum scar

sulphates   bromide   yellow spar

lime mudstone oxides isoteline trilobite   catastrophic

mud blanketing

during major prehistoric storms

The cabs of the trucks are covered. The drivers cough.

The red desert, how Antonioni saw the soul: shocked into color, blue smoke stack billowing yellow soot; permanent rust on a quarantine ship that can never dock, because, among the passengers, are no lovers who would want to sail forever.

At the edge of the vanished river, orange stain on the tree stumps, the heavy blue sky, water in mirages as black as oil although none of the area is now fed by it in any form. Y2K census: fewer than two hundred inhabitants.

Then the trucks, driving along the wind, veer around Dallas and scream down to the gulf.

There is a story about the poet Paul Carroll, around the time of the *Big Table* anthology, at a party in Chicago. He had gone out the back door of the apartment to the landing, and someone had locked the door after him. He knocked and banged and called out that he was in Dante's hell, but the people at the party refused to let him back in.

Sometimes when I hold the second cat up to my face, she puffs against my skin something warm that smells both spicy and dusty, like nice well-groomed fur, but the second cat isn't aware of me. She stretches elegantly, removes the grit from between her claws with her little tongue, orders her fur so it is plump, but she does not try to read my face

When the first cat became too ill to drink water, my daughter had to name the time her friend would be taken. Although the thin creature could still put her paw against your hand, she was too weak to push. The last moment began to close. Aftertime stretched, ashen. Ash (1) ON *askr* IE *osen* LAT *ornus* mountain ash; any of a group of timber and shade trees belonging to the olive family having pinnate leaves winged fruit and tough elastic wood with a straight close grain suited for the haft of hammers axes spears (2) ME *asche* akin to ON *askr;* the gray or silvery powder left by something after burning this color pallor.

> Pinnate leaves   drought
> wind thirst pallor
>   the Pelian ash spear against which
>   Achilles leaned thoughtfully when Athena
> promised him Hector

Looking Forth

From the room's shade:

sunflat ash trunks
                                   the vertical gray
of hitting your head
            against the color

behind which birds   at random depth
call far far
                        then near
all calls edged with oddity
like reverberations
in a tube

The sound of the unceasing traffic
                whole   headlong   surging
                    at the air
                                                    twines the moment
            against a nerve

Might peace come
                by withdrawing the eye
from the sound

                        in its fresh
                            calm

                                                there

            my daughter would be

                            unworried

            and there like the roll of prongs
                            in a player piano

all the clear times we would
                    stand in the middle of
            when it was summer

                                and my parents would appear
                smiling a little
            making ten thousand steps each day
                    before they became so old

even myself
                        in what state?
my mind full
of what it never filled with

                at just the right moment
                        (complete as solitude

hereness

gray runneled
                flecked with sunny lichen
            groomed by the tiny woodpeckers who
                    dance upwards
                hurling their heads against the bark

Acknowledgments

I am grateful to the National Humanities Center, and to my colleagues there, for the fellowship year during which I brooded over the works in this book.

Many thanks to the publications in which the following first appeared:

American Poetry Review: "Like a Furnace"
Henrik Ibsen Centenary (ed. Georges Mazur): "Brand"
Massachusetts Review: "Facing North"
The New Yorker: "First Passion"
Paris Review: "The Water-brooks"
Poetry: "Mountain View," "Claremont Raga," "At the In and Out," "Vigil," "The Poems I Am Not Writing," "Sale," "Mantid," "Looking Forth"
Salmagundi: "A Parakeet"
Southwest Review: "Privilege"

A NOTE ABOUT THE AUTHOR

California Sorrow is the seventh collection by Mary Kinzie, whose earlier volumes include *Drift, Autumn Eros,* and *Summers of Vietnam.* She is the literary executor of American poet Louise Bogan, and the author of *A Poet's Guide to Poetry.*

A NOTE ON THE TYPE

The text of this book was set in Walbaum, a typeface designed by Justus Erich Walbaum in 1810. Walbaum was active as a typefounder in Goslar and Weimar from 1799 to 1836. Though the letter forms of this face are patterned closely on the "modern" cuts then being made by Giambattista Bodoni and the Didot family, they are of a far less rigid cut. Indeed, it is the slight but pleasing irregularities in the cut that give this typeface its humane quality and account for its wide appeal. In its very appearance Walbaum jumps boundaries, having a look more French than German.

Composed by Creative Graphics,
Allentown, Pennsylvania

Printed and bound by Thomson-Shore, Inc.,
Dexter, Michigan

Designed by Soonyoung Kwon